TUTANKHAMUN

THE GOLDEN KING AND THE GREAT PHARAOHS

A SOUVENIR BOOK

ZAHI HAWASS

with photography by

SANDRO VANNINI

NATIONAL GEOGRAPHIC

WASHINGTON, D.C.

INTRODUCTION

WELCOME TO THE INCREDIBLE WORLD of Tutankhamun and the great pharaohs of ancient Egypt. Now that you have enjoyed the exhibition, you will carry many memories, and perhaps some questions, away with you, which is why we created this souvenir book for you. I put a lot of thought into choosing the objects to be shown in this book, asking myself which artifacts would be the best ones for you to take home to help you remember the experience of *Tutankhamun and the Golden Age of the Pharaohs.* It was a difficult decision, because each artifact in the exhibition has its own exciting story.

Clearly we would include treasures from the spectacular burial of the golden boy himself. But I have also chosen to include some of the objects that I discovered during my own adventures in archaeology.

The first is a group of statues of a man named Inty-shedu, a workman who helped build the pyramids of Giza. When you look into the eyes of these still vibrant images, you may feel as though you have been transported 4,500 years into the past. You catch a glimpse of the lives and spirit

CANOPIC STOPPERS carved and painted with Tutankhamun's image, these enclosed four miniature coffins placed inside the king's canopic chest to hold his organs.

THE PRIEST KAI gazes intently, his body limestone, his eyes calcite with pupils of inlaid crystal. Figures of his son and daughter peek out by his feet.

of the people who labored to construct these great monuments.

When I found these four statues, they were inside a hidden chamber in Inty-shedu's tomb. The largest one was in the middle, with two others to its left and one to its right. I felt that something was missing: The Egyptians loved symmetry, and I would have expected to see two small statues on each side of the larger one. When I searched carefully, I did indeed find the remains of a fifth statue: Made of wood, it had disintegrated almost completely.

On the day that we planned a press conference to announce the discovery of these unique statues, I was sitting in my office at Giza, waiting for the journalists to arrive. The ground began to shake, and I realized that we were experiencing an earthquake. As soon as the quake stopped, I ran from my office to check on the monuments—first the Sphinx, because at that time we were working to restore a piece of the colossal statue's shoulder, and then the statues of Inty-shedu, to be sure they were still safe in his tomb.

We did have to postpone the press conference, but after a few days, it was time to try again. I got up the morning of the rescheduled conference and got into the car next to my driver. In the middle of the trip from my apartment to the pyramids, I fainted. My driver took me straight to the hospital on the Pyramids Road, where the doctors found that I had suffered a heart attack. It certainly seemed that the curse of Inty-shedu was at work!

Another one of my discoveries that is included in this exhibition is the statue of the priest Kai and his children. I found this statue concealed behind the false door inside Kai's tomb at Giza. I will never forget how I felt when I peered through the holes in the false door, and saw the eyes of Kai gazing back at me. The moment when I first held this exquisite statue in my hands will remain in my memory forever. It is one of the best private statues to have survived from the Old Kingdom.

I have spent most of my life working at Giza, revealing the secrets of the pyramids and the Great Sphinx. I have chosen to include the statue of Khafre in this book to remind you that the Great Sphinx was carved as part of his pyramid complex.

Some have claimed that the monuments of Giza belonged to a lost civilization and were created thousands of years before the Old Kingdom. That idea is completely untrue, but it was once quite popular, and many people believed it. Egyptologists gave the theory no credence at all, and most would have preferred to ignore it. I knew, though, that we could not hide behind our books and allow the public to be misled by the people who were promoting this false version of history. I felt that I had to face the problem myself. So I held a series of debates with them, which helped many people hear and understand the truth.

The adherents of the lost civilization theory repeatedly requested permission to drill holes in the ground around the Sphinx, insisting that something was hidden underneath the ground. Strict government regulations made it impossible for us to allow

this, in spite of the fact that the media put great pressure on us to do so. Recently, however, we realized that the rising water table in front of the Sphinx Temple might be threatening the statue.

The experts supervising the project advised us to drill holes in front of the Sphinx and into its back to determine the actual water level. We bored five small holes, each about 70 feet deep, hitting the water table about 15 feet below the surface. We found nothing but solid rock all the way down—absolutely no evidence for lost civilizations at Giza or secret chambers hidden beneath the Sphinx.

The golden treasures from the tomb of Tutankhamun that are featured in these pages are truly amazing. They bring to life the thrill of Howard Carter's discovery of the tomb on November 4, 1922. I hope that history may repeat itself soon: I am very fortunate to be leading the first all-Egyptian team ever to excavate in the Valley of the Kings, and I believe that we will soon uncover a new tomb, which will be given the number KV64. I hope that even as you read this book, you will be hearing great news from the valley.

The circumstances that my team and I have met with in the Valley of the Kings are much like those that Howard Carter faced more than 85 years ago. When Carter found it, the entrance to Tutankhamun's tomb was covered by a layer of limestone chips and the remains of ancient workmen's huts dating from the period of the construction of the tomb of Ramesses IV, with additional rubble on top. In the same way, we found huge blocks of stone that had fallen from above, covering an area not far from the tomb of Tutankhamun.

When we moved these stones, we found an artificially smoothed cliff face and a flight of stairs leading down to what I believe to be a tomb, as yet undiscovered. I only hope that it is intact. If it is, the valley will once again be filled with life, just as it was in 1922 when

FOUR FIGURINES all represent Inty-shedu, a master builder of the pyramids at Giza. Buried in his tomb together, they signify his importance in his time.

THE SCRIBE HAPY, a steward of Amun from the 19th-dynasty reign of Ramesses, was shown with a pen in his right hand. His raised leg suggests he is reading.

Carter and his team began their work in the tomb of the golden boy.

I have been lucky enough to encounter the young pharaoh in person three times. The first time was in 2005, when I brought a CT scanner to the Valley of the Kings to examine his mummy. We learned that he was about 19 when he died, and we found no evidence that he had been murdered: The hole at the back of his head, identified by some as the cause of his death, was made by embalmers in the 18th dynasty. We did, however, find an unhealed fracture in his left leg, which suggests that he had an accident only a day or so before he died.

The second time that I met Tutankhamun was on November 4, 2007. On that day, we moved the fragile mummy of the golden boy to a state-of-the-art, climate-controlled display case within his tomb in the Valley of the Kings. This new case will protect and preserve his remains while allowing the public to see his face for the first time in history.

My most recent encounter with the golden boy, Tutankhamun, took place this year, when I went with a team of experts to take samples of his mummy for DNA testing in the hope that we will be able to identify more members of the young king's family and solve some of the mysteries that have long puzzled Egyptologists.

We took samples from a skeleton believed to be Akhenaten's that was found in another burial in the royal valley, KV55. We have also taken samples from the mummy of Akhenaten's father, Amenhotep III, along with those of Yuya and Tjuya, the parents of Amenhotep III's great queen, Tiye. We have done CT scans of two mummified fetuses that were found in Tutankhamun's tomb. I do hope that they prove to be the children of the golden boy, because this might enable us to identify the woman who was most likely their mother, Queen Ankhesenamun. If we were able to do this, it might in turn lead us to the mummy of Ankhesenamun's mother, Queen Nefertiti. I believe that the world will be amazed when we reveal the results of our research into the family of Tutankhamun. Perhaps we will finally be able to write the

TWO MAJOR GODS of the New Kingdom, Amun-Re and Re-Horakhty, sit side by side. Prayers on the back address Amun-Re as "lord of the sky, lord of the land," and Re-Horakhty as "the mighty falcon in the forefront" of the sun god's boat.

conclusion to the drama of the kings and queens of Amarna.

It seems that the magic of Tutankhamun will never end. A few months ago, I entered the Treasury of his tomb, where the Anubis shrine was discovered. I found that Howard Carter had left some objects inside, including seal impressions from both the interior and exterior doors of the tomb. Along with the emblem of the necropolis, a jackal above the nine bows that symbolized Egypt's enemies, some of these seal impressions bear the king's earlier name, Tutankhaten, while others bear the name Tutankhamun.

Inside a storage magazine on the West Bank at Luxor, we found a number of other objects left behind by Carter's team. I found it particularly interesting to see old copies of the London *Times*, which the team members read every day because it was the newspaper to which Carter's patron Lord Carnarvon had given the exclusive right to cover the discovery.

And our encounters with Tutankhamun have not been confined to the south of Egypt: Far to the north of Luxor, near the ancient city of Memphis, we recently found stone blocks dating to the reign of the boy king. One shows Tutankhamun smiting his enemies, while another shows him seated in the company of his wife. Part of a "window of appearances," where the king used to stand to give out rewards to his officials, can be seen on the second block. I believe that these reliefs indicate that Tutankhamun had a palace at Memphis.

I know that the legend of the golden boy will fascinate people all over the world for years to come. I am hoping that my excavations in the Valley of the Kings will reveal another intact tomb, bringing some of the glory of the pharaohs into today's world. Very soon, I do believe that we will see long-hidden treasures of gold and silver, "wonderful things" like those that Howard Carter found so many years ago. Let us hope that we do not encounter any ancient curses at the same time!

THUTMOSE III OFFERING NU-JARS is an exquisite 18th-dynasty figure of an ancestor of Tutankhamun. Some scholars suspect that this sculpture is a fake.

TUTANKHAMUN FLANKED BY DEITIES, a mural painting from the south wall of the boy king's tomb, shows his welcome to the afterlife by Anubis (left), the jackal-headed god of mummification, and Hathor, mistress of the western land, where the sun set and the dead were buried.

THE KINGS *of* EGYPT

THERE IS EVIDENCE OF HUMAN INHABITATION in Egypt as early as 700,000 to 500,000 B.C. By about 5300 B.C., the Egyptians had established some permanent farming communities on the edge of the desert that extended on either side of the fertile river valley. Distinct cultures can be traced in the Nile Delta to the north and in the Nile Valley to the south. The first evidence for writing, found in a tomb at the southern site of Abydos, dates from about 3150 B.C. By this time, kings were beginning to emerge.

By Dynasty 3, Egyptian kings were building step pyramids, considered stairs by which the king would climb to the stars after death. The king was the chief leader of the state, religious institutions, and military. In life he served as an intermediary between humankind and the many Egyptian divinities, and in death he became a god. The word "pharaoh" comes from a Hebrew word in the Old Testament referring to the ruler of Egypt, derived from an ancient phrase, *per aa,* meaning "great house." It was not used until much later in Egyptian history.

KHAFRE, A KING DURING DYNASTY 4, sits on a throne in this calcite sculpture, discovered at Mit Rahina in Memphis, Egypt's royal center during the Old Kingdom.

The New Kingdom, beginning with Dynasty 18 and dating from about 1569 to 1081 B.C., was the golden age of ancient Egypt. In this period Ahmose I laid the groundwork for Egypt's great empire to the northeast. He was succeeded by his son, Amenhotep I, and then two pharaohs named Thutmose. Thutmose II's great queen, Hatshepsut, promoted herself to full power as a pharaoh. Her stepson, Thutmose III, called the Napoleon of ancient Egypt, campaigned in Palestine and Syria, consolidating an empire that stretched north to the Euphrates River and south to the Fourth Cataract of the Nile. New Kingdom rulers used their resources to maintain a strong army and build enduring monuments. The Thutmosid line continued through the reign of the boy king, Tutankhamun.

Tutankhamun died without an heir, as did his two successors. A new dynasty, the 19th, began with Ramesses I. Ramesses II built all over Egypt. The last great warrior of the New Kingdom was Ramesses III, who died

AMENEMHAT III, represented in gray granite, and his father, Senwosret III, reigned through a long, stable period of the Middle Kingdom's Dynasty 12.

THIS UNUSUAL BLOCK STATUE depicting Hetep, who probably served in the court of Amenemhat I, presented many surfaces for carving hieroglyphic inscriptions.

AMENHOTEP III'S JEWELRY BOX, made of gilded wood, faience tile, and copper, was discovered in 1907 in KV 46, a small undecorated chamber in the Valley of the Kings. An inscription around the box confirms "Life, Stability, and Dominion."

a victim of a conspiracy hatched from within his own harem. Gradually Egypt lost its power over other nations. Far to the south, the Nubian kingdom of Kush gained in strength and by 732 B.C. had overtaken Egypt.

In the sixth century B.C. a new threat arose to the northeast, and Egypt was subject to Persian domination for the next two centuries, with only brief periods of native rule. Alexander the Great defeated the Persians in 332 B.C., and took over Egypt. Alexander's general, Ptolemy, proclaimed himself pharaoh. He and his descendants ruled from the city of Alexandria and ruled Egypt for nearly three centuries. In 30 B.C., the last of the Ptolemies, Cleopatra VII, lost the great sea battle of Actium to Octavius (Augustus Caesar), and Egypt became a Roman province.

A PIECE OF PAVEMENT from a New Kingdom palace, made of painted plaster, evokes geese flying up out of marshy grasses along the banks of the Nile.

SHABAQA (above), represented in this colossal head of pink granite, ruled during Dynasty 25, also called the Kushite or Nubian dynasty. His empire extended from today's central Sudan to the Mediterranean Sea.

SANDSTONE SCULPTURES of Amenhotep IV including this one stood against large square pillars in the colonnade of the king's temple to the god Aten at East Karnak. His double crown signifies that the living king is also a representative of the sun god.

AMENHOTEP III (at left), an 18th-dynasty pharaoh, wears the "blue crown" signifying his divine kingship, but his head is painted mysteriously red, perhaps for reasons of ritual magic.

LARGER THAN LIFE, only the upper part remains of a granodiorite statue of Ramesses II, a 19th-dynasty pharaoh, who is shown wearing a round wig decorated in front with a uraeus—a cobra—and in back with sun disks, both symbols of power

ZAHI HAWASS examines a group of Greco-Roman mummies that were laid to rest in a family tomb in the Valley of the Golden Mummies, a vast necropolis in the Bahariya Oasis.

PHARAOH'S HOUSEHOLD

THE PHARAOH USUALLY HAD MANY WIVES, one of whom had chief status and sometimes took the title "daughter of the god." Close intermarriage occurred among royalty, and multiple wives provided a group of potential heirs to continue the perpetuation of the family line. Like the pharaoh, the royal women had specific titles and regalia, and they received similar, if not as elaborate, burials.

Queens sometimes played important roles in the administration of the country, and women ruled the country at key points in Egyptian history. For example, Hatshepsut not only ruled Egypt, she claimed the throne in her own name as pharaoh, adopted male regalia, and had others refer to her in the masculine gender. Nefertiti had a temple devoted entirely to her and may even have succeeded her husband, Akhenaten, to the throne.

Although the evidence is scanty, it seems that succession was ensured, whenever possible, through the direct line established by the eldest son of the king and his chief queen. If the principal consort of the king bore only female children, it appears that one of these daughters would marry the son

KEY FEATURES of this 18th-dynasty fragment—the dress, the collar, the beads, and the wig—suggest that the woman represented belonged to a royal family.

of a minor wife, and this prince would become the next king. It was also possible, as in the case of Thutmose III, for oracles to legitimize a successor. There are also examples of co-regencies—cases in which the king would select and crown his heir during his own lifetime—and in those circumstances the two kings would reign together. This arrangement guaranteed a smooth transition of power at the senior king's death. Not surprisingly, we know of a number of instances when the transfer of the throne was contested.

The royal family resided in a palace, which also served as a space for the enactment of rituals, ceremonies, state occasions, and diplomatic events. Some later palaces included gardens and pools. Kings usually had more than one residence, while queens and occasionally princesses could have their own palaces. The royal children were brought up in these buildings, with special nurses and tutors assigned to them. The principal queen, the queen mother, and the royal children shared in the divinity of the king and played important ritual roles.

QUEEN NOFRET, the consort of the 12th-dynasty pharaoh Senwosret II, wears a heavy banded wig topped with a royal insignia, the rearing cobra.

BELONGING TO QUEEN MERERET, the 12th-dynasty daughter of Senwosret III, this necklace is made of elongated beads of gold, lapis lazuli, and carnelian, separated by round golden spacers. Across it a vulture goddess, mistress of heaven, spreads her wings.

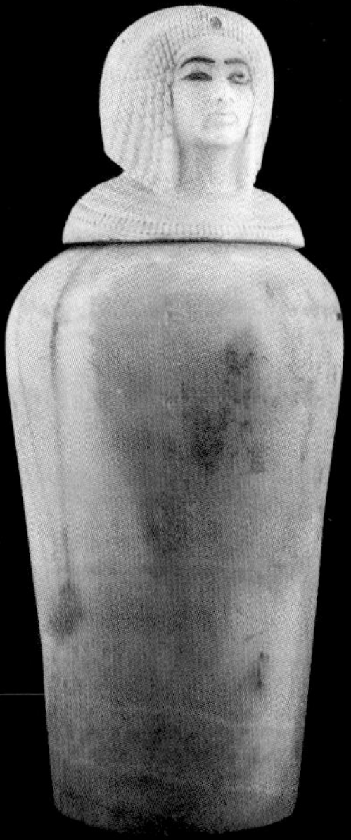

INTIMATIONS OF DOMESTICITY, here are a sculpture of a princess and her caretaker, a canopic jar that may have belonged to a royal, and a sarcophagus for a high priest's cat. All represent New Kingdom works, from Dynasty 18, but each reflects a different leadership. Senenmut (left) holds Princess Neferure, daughter of Queen Hatshepsut. The owner of the tomb that included the canopic jar (above) may have been Akhenaten or his mother. The cat belonged to Thutmose, son of Amenhotep III.

QUEEN HATSHEPSUT kneels to make an offering to the gods in this granite figure. A rare female pharaoh, she is here represented as wearing the royal kilt and headdress more often worn by male pharaohs.

LIKE MANY PRINCESSES, Shepenwepet II, daughter of a 25th-dynasty pharaoh in the early seventh century B.C., served as a high priestess and received the titles of divine adoratress and god's wife of Amun.

THE IDENTITY of this royal woman is uncertain. She is normally considered to be a king's daughter, since her bald head could suggest youth, but the head is of an adult woman and has much in common with representations of Nefertiti.

THE TOMB OF MERESANKH III, with its beautifully decorated chapel, was built for the granddaughter of King Khufu, who became the queen of his son Khafre. This tomb lies east of the Great Pyramid, in a cemetery dedicated to Khufu's family.

PHARAOH'S RELIGION

THE PHARAOH WAS THE INCARNATION of the divine on earth, the terrestrial representative of the gods. He was also, especially after death, counted as one of the gods himself. At the same time, he was the human high priest of every god, responsible for proper care of the gods worshipped in the many state temples built throughout the country.

The worship of Re, the sun god, was the principal cult for the Egyptians from early in their history. The pyramid was a symbol for this god. The daily solar cycle was thought to echo the cycle of life, with sunset paralleling death and sunrise paralleling resurrection. Thus Re, the sun god, is associated with cyclical, eternally repeating time.

The myth of Osiris is one of the oldest in Egyptian history. It tells of the triumph of good over evil and conveys the belief that death was a transition to a different state of being. Osiris represented fertility and the flood. If the flood was low, it meant that Osiris was dead; when the water level became higher, it meant that Osiris was coming back to life. Thus the god Osiris is linked with linear time, time with a beginning and, eventually, an end.

THE GOD SOPDU, protector of Egypt's borders with foreign lands, was represented in writing and here in sculpture as a seated hawk. Sopdu also assumed human form.

THIS LEOPARD'S FACE decorated a robe worn by priests who performed an important funerary ritual called the Opening of the Mouth. Dressed as a leopard, the officiant magically "opened" the eyes, nose, ears, and mouth of the mummy, preparing for judgment by Osiris. The ritual preceded final burial.

Osiris became the king of the netherworld, and Egyptians believed that after a king died, he joined with Osiris at night and was reborn as Re in the morning. For that reason, the deceased king is often shown in the mummiform shape of Osiris. Texts were inscribed inside kings' burial suites, collections of spells believed to help the king reach the other world to meet Osiris.

For much of its 3,000-year history, Egyptian religion consisted of hundreds of deities, male and female, animal and human, and combinations of both. A few represented abstract elements, such as the wind, storms, the sky, the Earth, the sun, and the moon. Gods could have national or local scope, and sometimes they were syncretized, or combined into one, such as Amun-Re and Re-Horakhty. No single collection of doctrines, such as the Bible or the Koran, guided their beliefs, yet the Egyptians held a religious ideology consistently for millennia.

THE GOD DUAMUTEF, one of the four sons of Horus, bears a jackal's head and guards the stomach of the deceased in the passage to the afterlife.

PRIESTS WERE IMPORTANT OFFICIALS appointed to serve the state gods of ancient Egypt. Imhotep (at left) is known to have held priestly and administrative functions under Djoser in Dynasty 3, around 2600 B.C. Later a cult of Imhotep developed, its followers believing that he had special power to cure disease.

Ramessesnakht (near right) became high priest at Karnak during the reign of Ramesses VI. This sculpture shows him in his role as a scribe. Climbing on top of his head is a baboon, an animal associated with Thoth, patron god of scribes.

A Late Period standing statue of the god Osiris (far right) includes details linking him with the ruling pharaohs: the tall crown of Upper Egypt and the flail and crook in his crossed hands. By the time of this sculpture, the cult of Isis and Osiris attracted people seeking personal salvation.

THE GREAT PYRAMIDS at Giza were built as tombs for the 4th-dynasty kings Khufu, Khafre, and Menkaure, around 2500 B.C. Visible in the foreground are the small pyramids of Menkaure's queens.

GOLD *of the* PHARAOHS

ANCIENT EGYPT IS LEGENDARY FOR ITS WEALTH IN GOLD. It formed the basis for beautiful jewelry and was used to cover boxes, coffins, and statuettes. The bodies of the gods were made of gold, and gold could protect the deceased in the afterlife.

Gold first appears in the Egyptian archaeological record during the Badarian period, between 4500 and 3800 B.C. The oldest known source of gold was located near Qift (today's Coptos), where about 1,300 workmen's huts dating to the Old Kingdom have been found near an old gold mine. In the Middle Kingdom, the Egyptians expanded their goldfields south into Nubia, and they continued to use gold from the deserts of Kush and Wawat during the New Kingdom. In the reign of Amenhotep II, a load of gold from Kush required 150 men to carry it.

During the reign of Amenhotep II, gold explorations went as far away as a place called Karka, which may have been south of the Fourth Cataract of the Nile. A series of trading posts and fortresses, begun in the Middle Kingdom and expanded in the New Kingdom, protected those

A GLIMMERING MINIATURE, this coffinette of gold, carnelian, and colored glass rested inside Tutankhamun's canopic chest and held organs of the deceased pharaoh.

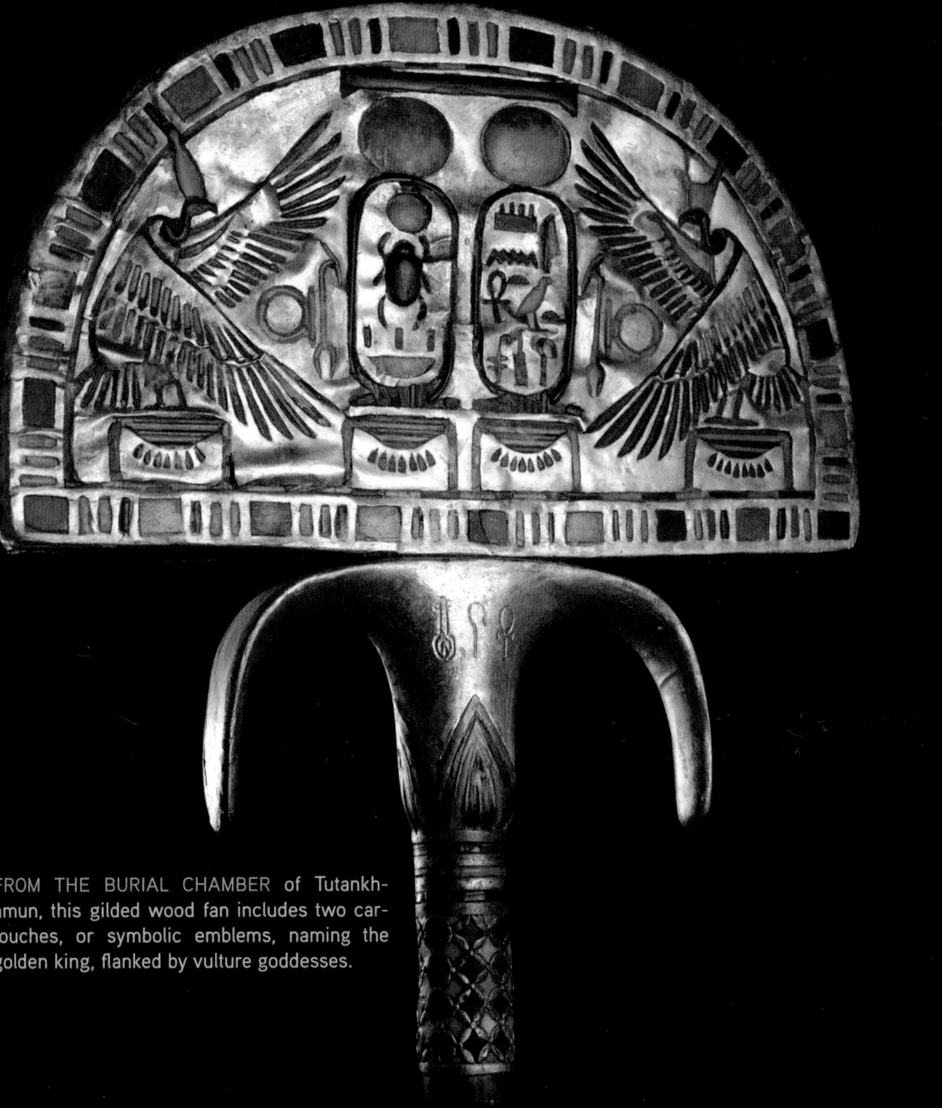

FROM THE BURIAL CHAMBER of Tutankhamun, this gilded wood fan includes two cartouches, or symbolic emblems, naming the golden king, flanked by vulture goddesses.

goldfields and trading routes. King Sety I himself visited the gold mines in the middle of the Eastern Desert. A map from the reign of Ramesses IV shows the location of gold mines during this period; now in the Turin Museum, it is considered the oldest geological map in the world.

To mine gold from veins of quartz, ancient Egyptians began by excavating large pieces of rock from underground. They pounded or ground the rock into a powder and rinsed the resulting material in order to separate the gold from its rock matrix.

The earliest scenes of goldsmithing are found in the tomb of Nebemakhet, which dates to Dynasty 4. During the New Kingdom, one supervisor of the royal goldsmiths was recorded as knowing the "secrets of the houses of gold," which meant that he knew how the statues of the gods, kept thoroughly hidden from any profane eyes, were made.

LOTUS PETALS, chased into this golden chalice, appear inside the cup as it is emptied. The name of Queen Tawosret is incised on the stem.

Gifts of gold were given to members of the royal family and to soldiers as a reward for bravery. Much of the gold jewelry found in tombs was probably worn by its owners in life and then buried with them for their enjoyment and protection in the afterlife. It indicated the wealth and status of the wearer. Gold was connected with the light of the sun, and just as the deceased had enjoyed sunlight during his lifetime, he could enjoy it after death by having gold buried with him.

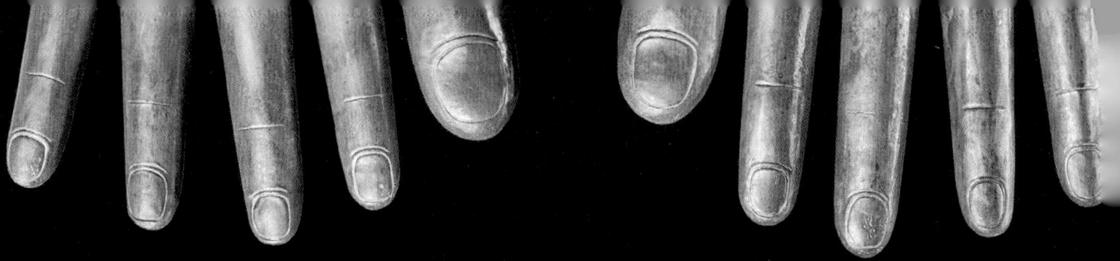

GOLDEN COVERS, or stalls, protected the fingers and toes of the mummy of Tutankhamun. Serving a magical function similar to amulets, they guarded the king's extremities from dangers as he traveled through the underworld.

For the ancient Egyptians, gold had miraculous power. The bodies of the gods were made of gold, and each piece of gold jewelry buried with a mummy performed a specific function. Even the poor buried their dead with yellow-colored beads in imitation of the gold believed to be so important for the passage into the afterlife.

Golden sandals adorned the young king's feet in his burial as well. The precious metal was inscribed with a texture similar to that of papyrus, of which everyday sandals would have been made.

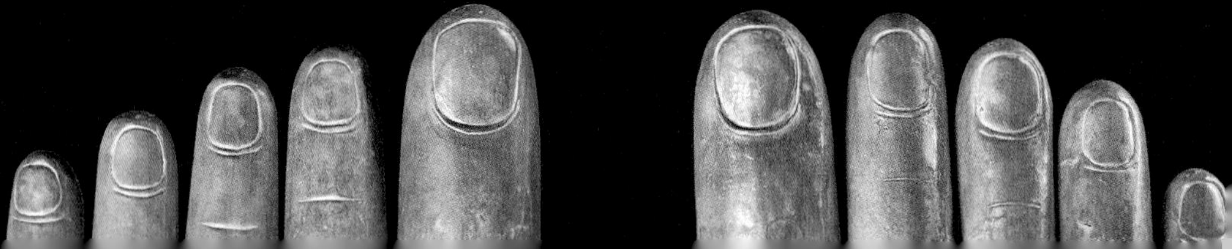

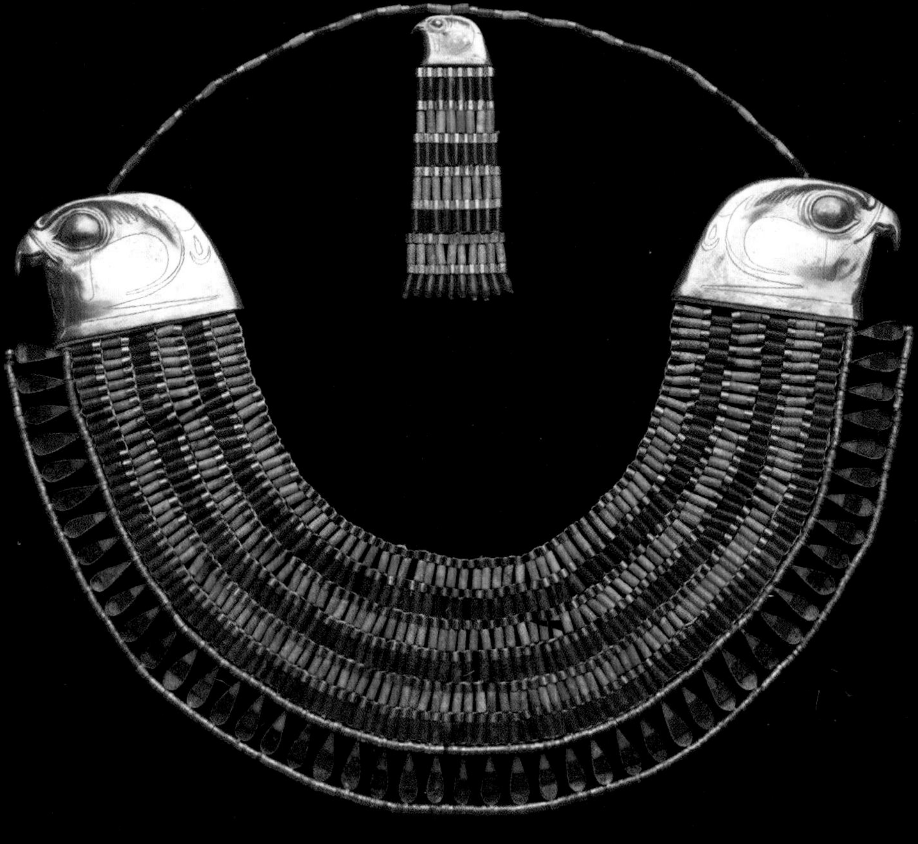

A COLLAR FOR A SPECIAL DAUGHTER, this intricate necklace of precious beads and gold falcon heads belonged to Neferuptah, daughter of the 12th-dynasty ruler Amenemhat III. She must have held an important place in his court, for a pyramid was built for her.

THIRTY ROWS OF TINY BEADS made of gold, carnelian, lapis lazuli, and turquoise, and every five rows includes a triangle: The geometries of this New Kingdom bracelet may represent rhythms of the lunar calendar. The spouted vessel (right), while found in the 21st-dynasty tomb of Psusennes I, was probably made in the 18th dynasty—a valued heirloom.

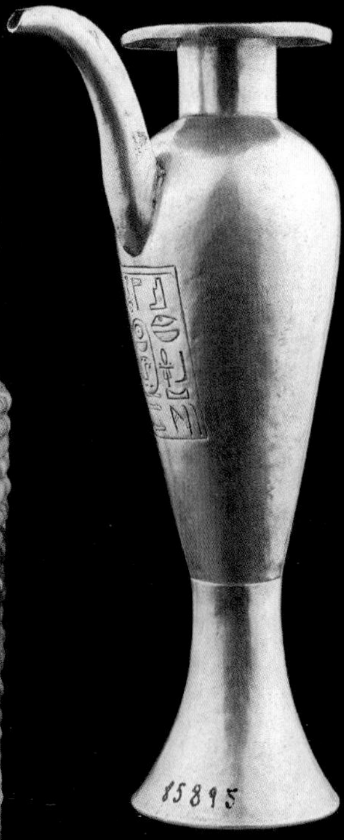

THE TOMB OF MENTUEMHAT dates from the Late Period of ancient Egyptian history. Found in the Assasif, an area on the Nile's west bank, it belongs to a group that includes the largest and most magnificent sepulchers in the Theban necropolis.

THE DISCOVERY *of a* PHARAOH

FOR ALMOST 3,000 YEARS, THE TOMB of Tutankhamun lay secret and undiscovered. Robbers had entered the chambers shortly after the young king's burial, but officials saved some of the treasures buried with him and resealed the tomb. Tutankhamun's short reign, the elimination of his name from official records due to his association with the revolutionary ruler Akhenaten, and the appropriation of his monuments by his successors all helped to maintain his obscurity and keep his tomb unknown for millennia.

With the 20th century came explorers intent on finding this lost tomb. One explorer, British archaeologist Howard Carter, succeeded. Aided by his patron, Lord Carnarvon, he searched an area he had determined would yield results. It took several long expeditions over a period of years before he realized his goal, discovering an almost intact royal tomb.

On November 4, 1922, Carter found a carved stairway and a corridor leading to a sealed doorway. As he peered in, the contents of the chamber beyond came into view: gilded chariots, shrines with figures of ancient

TUT'S GILDED WOOD SHABTI, found in the Annex of his tomb, was inscribed with text stating that its task was to rise up and work on behalf of the deceased pharaoh.

Egypt's deities inside, shimmering statues, coffered food supplies, the young king's bed, gilded funerary couches, ornately carved and inlaid furniture, elaborate stone vessels, covered chests with unknown contents, and more—the treasures piled one upon the other, almost from floor to ceiling. "Can you see anything?" his patron asked.

"Yes, wonderful things," he replied.

At the end of the Antechamber, two life-size statues of Tutankhamun flanked a sealed doorway. Thieves from centuries past had entered the room but had not succeeded in violating Tutankhamun's mummy. Intact, it lay within four huge gilded wooden shrines, each inscribed with protective magical spells, inside a stone sarcophagus. Two gilded wooden coffins and a solid golden coffin provided additional security. Tutankhamun had survived the millennia.

It took more than ten years for Carter to search, photograph, record, and conserve

FIVE PAIRS OF EARRINGS were found in the tomb of Tutankhamun, including these with a duck head and wings in the center and five cobras hanging below.

the 5,000 objects and more found in the Antechamber, the Annex, the Treasury, and the Burial Chamber of Tutankhamun's tomb. He unwrapped the mummy for study, then replaced it in sand inside the sarcophagus.

X-rays were first taken of Tutankhamun in 1968. When the Egyptian parliament agreed to send some of Tut's treasures abroad for the first time in almost 25 years, I decided this would be a good opportunity to use new technology to reexamine the mummy. On January 5, 2005, I looked upon Tutankhamun's face for the first time. Using a portable CT-scanning machine, we produced 1,700 computer-enhanced three-dimensional images of the golden king. Our research concluded that Tutankhamun died at the age of about 19, but not by a blow to the head, which had long been theorized.

THIS SIMPLE BED, one of seven found in the tomb of Tutankhamun, may have been used by the golden king during his lifetime as well.

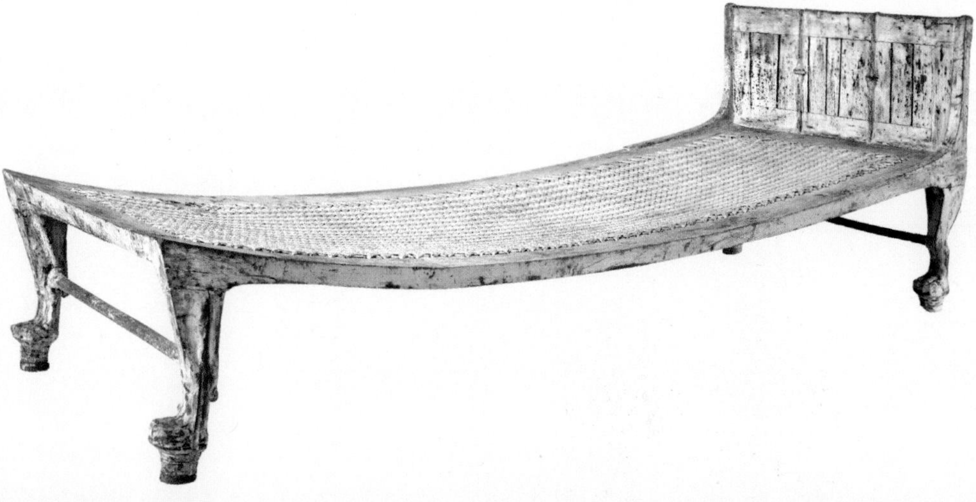

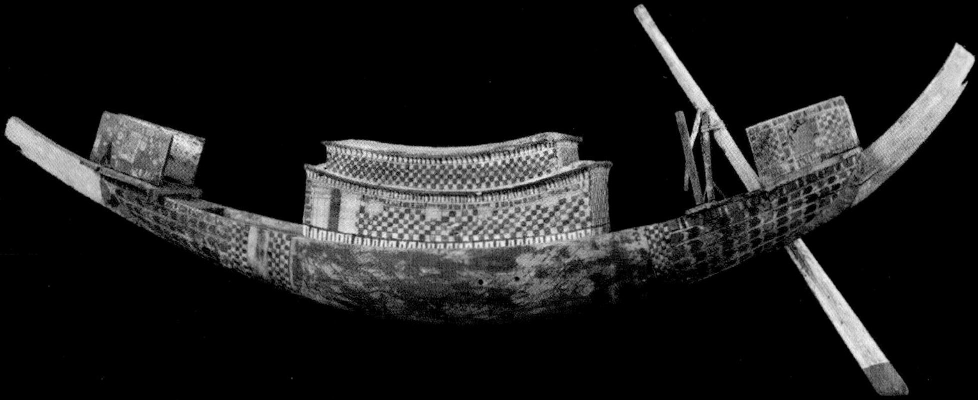

OBJECTS FOUND IN THE TOMB of Tutankhamun shed light on ancient Egyptian beliefs about the afterlife.

As many as 18 model boats, including the one above, were discovered in the Treasury. Many have intricate decorations and inscriptions on them, suggesting the symbolism of a vessel that carries the dead on their pilgrimage to Abydos, the mythical burial place of the god Osiris, and to other sacred sites. Tomb paintings and murals likewise depicted journeys by boat.

Jewelry was believed to hold powers that could protect against evil. A necklace with three scarabs (right) was discovered within the wrappings of Tutankhamun's mummy. This piece contains many magical elements, including the three gold disks. The outer two signify the sun and the middle one, cradled in a crescent, signifies the moon.

THIS IVORY GAME BOX with a drawer to hold playing pieces was one of four found in Tutankhamun's tomb. One surface of the box provides the board for a game called tjau. Flipped over, the box's opposite surface provides the board for another game, called senet.

FORMED IN THREE LAYERS, this decorated unguent vessel contains a thin lining sitting inside a thicker shell with openwork between them, carved in patterns with intricate symbolism. It was one of many vessels found in Tutankhamun's tomb.

The band of openwork decoration is composed of three vignettes. In two of them, winged cobras perch atop signs that stand for gold and support the king's cartouches, or signature lozenges. At their backs is the ankh-sign, symbol of life. In the third, a winged scarab supports the disk of the sun with its forelegs.

THE TOMB OF TUTANKHAMUN contained a remarkable number of chairs. This one, made of wood and painted white, contains many details that offer magical powers and protection to the pharaoh: its legs shaped like those of a lion; its back carved to show the god Horus as a falcon and, below the falcon's wings, the ankh-sign, symbol of life.

Some of the chairs in the tomb, including this one, were probably made specifically as funerary furniture, but others—including small, child-size chairs—may have been used in daily life.

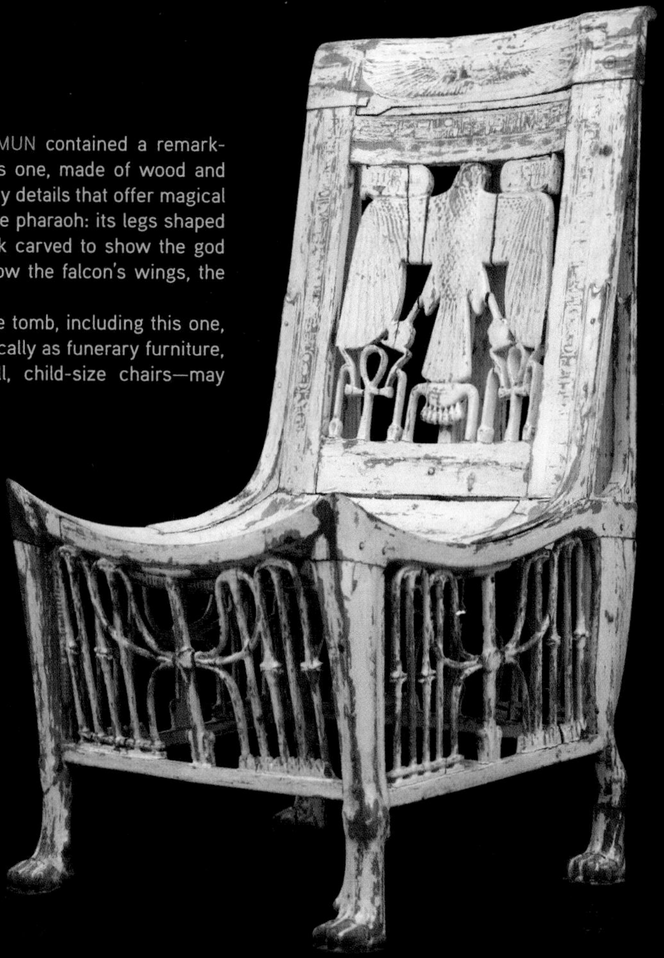

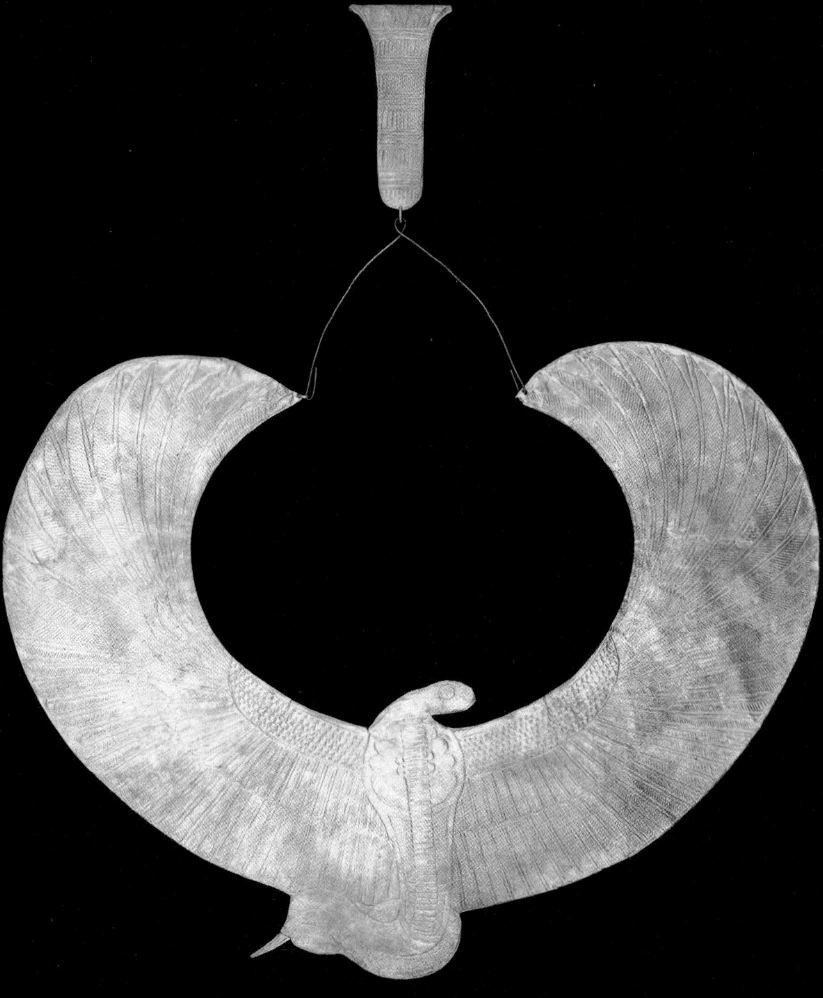

A WINGED COBRA animates this gold collar, found within the wrappings of the young king's mummy. The wing tips are pierced with tiny holes for the wire by which the collar was suspended around the mummy's neck. A sheet of gold, shaped like an elongated lotus blossom, hangs from the wire in counterpoise.

Larger than life, the colossal statue of Tutankhamun (right) is one of a pair found at the remains of the funerary temple of Ay and Horemheb on the west bank of Thebes near Medinet Habu. (The other is at the University of Chicago.)

King Tutankhamun was only about 19 years old when he died without an heir. His young wife may have suspected that one of his high officials, Ay or Horemheb, had conspired to murder him. Ay ruled for a few years after Tut's death. Then Horemheb, commander in chief of the army, took the throne, and eventually usurped many of Tut's monuments, such as this statue.

TUTANKHAMUN

THE GOLDEN KING AND THE GREAT PHARAOHS

ZAHI HAWASS

PUBLISHED BY THE NATIONAL GEOGRAPHIC SOCIETY

John M. Fahey, Jr., *President and Chief Executive Officer*
Gilbert M. Grosvenor, *Chairman of the Board*
Tim T. Kelly, *President, Global Media Group*
John Q. Griffin, *President, Publishing*
Nina D. Hoffman, *Executive Vice President;*
President, Book Publishing Group

PREPARED BY THE BOOK DIVISION

Kevin Mulroy, *Senior Vice President and Publisher*
Leah Bendavid-Val, *Director of Photography Publishing and Illustrations*
Marianne R. Koszorus, *Director of Design*
Barbara Brownell Grogan, *Executive Editor*
Elizabeth Newhouse, *Director of Travel Publishing*

STAFF FOR THIS BOOK

Susan Tyler Hitchcock, *Project and Text Editor*
Dana Chivvis and Kevin Eans, *Illustrations Editors*
Melissa Farris, *Art Director*
Richard S. Wain, *Production Manager*

Jennifer A. Thornton, *Managing Editor*
Gary Colbert, *Production Director*
Meredith C. Wilcox, *Administrative Director, Illustrations*

MANUFACTURING AND QUALITY MANAGEMENT

Christopher A. Liedel, *Chief Financial Officer*
Phillip L. Schlosser, *Vice President*
Chris Brown, *Technical Director*
Nicole Elliott, *Manager*
Monika D. Lynde, *Manager*
Rachel Faulise, *Manager*

Founded in 1888, the National Geographic Society is one of the largest nonprofit scientific and educational organizations in the world. It reaches more than 285 million people worldwide each month through its official journal, *NATIONAL GEOGRAPHIC,* and its four other magazines; the National Geographic Channel; television documentaries; radio programs; films; books; videos and DVDs; maps; and interactive media. National Geographic has funded more than 8,000 scientific research projects and supports an education program combating geographic illiteracy.

For more information, please call 1-800-NGS LINE (647-5463) or write to the following address:

National Geographic Society
1145 17th Street N.W.
Washington, D.C. 20036-4688 U.S.A.

Visit us online at www.nationalgeographic.com

For rights or permissions inquiries, please contact National Geographic Books Subsidiary Rights: ngbookrights@ngs.org

Library of Congress Cataloging-in-Publication Data

Hawass, Zahi A.
Tutankhamun : the golden king and the great pharaohs : a souvenir book / Zahi Hawass ; with photographs by Sandro Vannini.
p. cm.
ISBN 978-1-4262-0490-6
1. Tutankhamen, King of Egypt--Tomb. 2. Egypt--Antiquities. 3. Egypt--Civilization--To 332 B.C. I. Vannini, Sandro. II. Title.
DT87.5.H387 2008
932'.014092--dc22
[B]

2008041745

ISBN 978-1-4262-0490-6

Printed in the U.S.A.